73

Barely Amazing

by Shane Koyczan

Write Bloody Publishing

writebloody.com

First edition.
ISBN: 978-0984503179

Cover Design by Derrick C. Brown
Interior Layout by Nikki Steele
Proofread by Wess Mongo Jolley
Author Photo by Kaare Iverson

Type set in Bergamo.

Printed in the USA

Write Bloody Publishing
Los Angeles, CA

Support Independent Presses
writebloody.com

[Dedication]

Barely Amazing

Barely Amazing

PREFACE

Some of the words in this book, pyjamas, favourite and more are not misspellings but rather Canadian versions of words commonly found in the United States.

Remember How We Forgot?

Remember how we forgot?

Remember how no one ever really
died in the wars we fought
because each gunshot
came from our fingertips
and we never really
kept them loaded
just in case?

Because each enemy was a friend
and none of it was about oil
religion or land it was all
just pretend.

Remember how we used to bend reality
like we were circus strongmen like
our imaginations were in shape then
and we were all ninjas trained in the
deadly art of
did not
like I totally got you
did not.

Remember how we forgot?

Remember how our parents told us
never to look directly into the son
and we were their sons so we
never looked directly into the mirror
in fear that we would go blind?

Remember how we used to find any old reason
just to call someone we were crushing on like
we could just pawn off our sense of embarrassment
and buy a chunk of courage
that would last just long enough
to have us asking them about math and stuff
and how stuff was just stuff like
I heard you're getting braces

and how braces somehow were
and still are
kinda hot?

Remember how we forgot?

Remember how we all caught mono
and folks would go *ohhh the kissing disease*
and how our first steps into gangsterhood
had us saying *mother please*
even though we'd never kissed anyone
even though we never did half the
things we'd said we'd done?

We spun yarns like
Rumpelstiltskin spun gold
we told ghost stories never knowing
we would one day ourselves be ghosts
haunting the hallways of schools
poltergeists breaking the rules
of silence in the library.

But we had no chains to rattle
no voice to battle the fact that we had
no vocal cords we had only fingernails
on chalkboards and they would scream
shout and yell trying to tell ourselves
what experience can teach
is what no teacher taught.

Remember how we forgot?

Once upon a time we were young
our dreams hung like apples waiting
to be picked and peeled as if
our hopes were something
needing to be reeled in so we could
finally fill the always empty big fish
bin of the one that got away
then proudly say that this time
impossible is not an option
because success is so akin to

effort and opportunity they
could be related.

So we took chances
we figure skated on thin ice we
believed each slice of life was served
with something sweet on the side
and failure was never nearly as important
as the fact that we tried.

That in the war against frailty and limitation
we supplied the determination it takes
to make ideas and goals the parents
of possibility and we believe ourselves
to be members of this family.

Not just one branch on one tree
but a forest whose roots
make up a dynasty.

So when I call you sis or bro
it's not lightly and when
I ask you to remember it's
because the future isn't
what it used to be.

So remember now.

Pay tribute to every sacrifice
laid upon the altar of somehow
for all the times somehow we overcame
                somehow we pushed on
                somehow we've gone the distance
and in going there we possess the freedom
to map the uncharted lands
of any and everywhere.

We are unbound.

Six feet above the underground
where we will all one day rest.

So until then test the limits
test the boundaries and borders
realize that the headquarters of potential
lay just beyond the world's edge.

Let the belief that hope belongs to us all
be the pledge you take to make the
unachievable as inconceivable
as the false fact that
we were never here.

We were here.

And our memories are
as dear to us as every slow-
motion moment or held breath.

So remember every instant before death
remember every first kiss
first dance near miss last chance
yes no maybe so.
Let us go the distance once more.

Let us remember all the moments
that were and were not
like the point is something we can
get and what we can get
is what we got
because all we have are the times
in between the moments
we connect each dot.

So live and remember
burn like an ember
capable of starting fires
like each moment inspires the next
like memories are the context
we put ourselves in so that life
becomes the next of kin we need
to notify in case of a big bang
or extinction level event.

Let now be our advent.

Live like we meant it
burn like we mean it
because this world doesn't give a shit
if we finish in a train wreck or car crash
if our story ends with a dot or a dash
if we were dust or ash

because all we were is all we'll
be because all we are is
the in between of
so far so good.

So forget every would could should not
    forget remembering how we forgot
live like a plot twist exist
now and in memory because
we burn bright.

Our light leaves scars on the sun
let no one say we will be undone by time's
passing the memories we are amassing
will stand as testament that somehow we
bent minds around the concept
that we see others in ourselves
that self-knowledge can't be found on bookshelves
so who we are has no bearing
on how we appear.

So look directly into every mirror
realize our reflections are
the first sentence of a story
and our story starts—

we were here.

Atlantis

Your entire body shakes when you laugh
as if your sense of humor was built on
a fault line and the coast of your heart
falls into the ocean of yourself.

And I'm left looking for this Atlantis.

Left looking for this place that exists
in stories told by old men who were
there when mathematics assured us
our willingness to believe was greater
than our determination
to dismiss.

I'm left looking for Atlantis
regardless of the scientists that
insist my efforts would be better spent
unearthing clues to where
the wild things went.

Try as it might faith can't put a dent in fact
so we must settle for watching science
re-enact the world as if the universe
was curled around this globe and if we
consider that the universe is never ending
then we're not even
a microbe.

We're like a death threat from a pacifist.

We're nothing.

But the Heisenberg Uncertainty Principle states
that nothing is faux shizzle and the
interesting thing about that is
it ensures the principle itself
can't even be a fact.

But we still act

as if this time we can see
the forest through the trees
regardless of the softwood lumber levies.
We fall in line like reforested pine
it's all straight rows where everything grows
a little less wild and a little
more humdrum ho hum.
We come from a mentality that rarely
sees the horror in symmetry
or the beauty in non-conformity.

We insist that for us
everything must be clear cut.
But what about philosophy?
What about the tree that fell in a forest
that no one was around to hear?
It's a little less clear
and a little more deep—
deep like if Donald Trump farts in a bathtub
and no bubbles come to the surface
is there an alternate universe where
the price of gas is cheap?

Possible but we can't prove it
any more than we can prove
that light can move fast enough
to stop a monster hiding in a closet.

We deposit our faith in fear
but clear our minds to the possibility
that maybe we as adults secretly sometimes
still get scared of the dark
and things that go bump
in the night.

And I can't prove I've ever loved anyone.

But despite the smoking and the overweight body
I want to grow old with you go through
muscle and joint pains to the point
that every time it rains
we can feel it in our knees.

We'd have arthritis so bad that
every time we make love we sound
like two bowls of Rice Krispies—
we're all snap crackle and pop.
But we still stop to take the time
and take the time.

I'm looking for Atlantis
letting faith turn this fiction into fact
as if I've tracked this missing continent
for decades and all I know so far is
that it's somewhere underwater.
I'm looking for clues
in those blurry photos of UFOs
and thinking if aliens are so smart then
why don't they start making their
spaceships look like airplanes?
That way we'd point to the sky and say
"an airplane how commonplace...
and not at all suspect."

We're all shipwrecked on this idea
that everything has to be explained
but maybe we just need to believe
that lemmings jump off of cliffs
to prove that they love us.

It's nice to believe that somebody out there
cares enough to plummet onto jagged back-
breaking rocks in an attempt to tell us
we're beautiful

                        tell us
that as far as life goes
our fingerprints are like snowflakes—
we leave them on everything but
they melt in the time it takes
to touch someone's tongue.
But if we're lucky
maybe we're remembered along with
the sunken cities of a lost continent.

This is for each child who is a monument
to the one who came before.

Maybe the best we can hope for
is that those we leave behind
find comfort in knowing
they were born out of love
and not science.

That biology explains *the how*
but love explains *the why*.

So in the event of our deaths
we hereby bequeath
all of these words to you
and they are only meant to say
that uncertainty is something
everyone goes through
and there's not much
in the way of proof but believe me
we loved you.

We held our breath
for your fist steps and your first word
laughed when it finally occurred
to you lemons are sour.

This is for every time love
becomes the finest minute
in the darkest hour.

This is for those who scour the streets
wondering where the wild things went
for the believers who lent us their madness
this is for everyone we miss
and this is for the children who were lost.

Sadness is nothing more than the cost
of being able smile once in a while
and grief is the trial we stand
to offer evidence that your fingerprints
were left on our hearts and our skin

and in terms of proof
love can be demonstrated
in giving.

Our lives consist of the efforts we give
in swimming toward a lost
continent where you are
rumoured to be living.

A Letter To Remind Me Who I Am

Dear Me…

This is you
               me.

Get up.

The ground is your reward
it will hold you when you are done.

Cancel all forks—
you are not done.

put a silencing finger to the lips
of all singing fat ladies.

This is not over.

Reel in all finish lines
steal the sound of the metal ringing
hanging in the air
and put it back in the bell—
one more round we go.

Get up.

There are sunsets that need to be
signed off on snowfalls that
need your approval
starry nights like sad lovers
whose beauty has gone unnoticed
in the glare of television sets.

They are looking for volunteers
to notice them
                    raise your hand
                    step forward
you will not be chastised for staring—
some beauty wants to be seen.

Get up.

As if the simple act of standing
has brought you closer to the cosmos
than you have ever previously been
as if all the stars you've seen
have been busy looking back
taking notes and keeping track
of which wishes need granting.

They heard you ask for strength
so show them you haven't wasted it.

Get up.

Despite gravity
with her magnetic arms
coaxing your metal dreams away
from flight despite everything that
will be said to weaken you against
the towering odds that stand
before you like a mountain
kissing vertigo into your grip
and daring you to look down.

Climb.

Not out of stubbornness
not out of a need to demonstrate
the depth of will it takes
to carry on but because
you owe you one.

You owe you one
for every second you ever spent
painting skulls onto white flags
and rescuing yourself from even
the option of surrender.

For every instant
you rebuilt your heart
using smiles salvaged from the grateful

faces of those who you reminded
how to laugh.

Now laugh.

Because one time in the middle of sex
she asked you to pretend you were a sea cow
and you did and it was then
as it is now
okay to laugh.

Your lungs will fill
like the bank accounts of the corrupt.

Your lungs will collapse
like backyard tents after
ghost stories and
strange noises.

Breathe.

Dear Me…
there will be another breath.

Dear Me…
silence is not a song
you should know all the words to.

Dear Me…
this is you.

Me.

Sidestep calamity like a matador
taking on a bullet.

Rise as if the sun has taken a day off
and hired you as it's substitute
leaving behind its lesson plan
and a world full of students
who can see no practical value
in what you are teaching.

Teach them.

Today's lesson is the same
as everyday before it
because the class has been
struggling with this assignment.

Shine.

You must teach this
by example.

So hand out sunglasses
and do not dim yourself
for the sake of their comfort.
The world is practiced in demanding
that those who can cast light
not do it with such radiance.

Show them the falling stars
dripping onto the horizon
like drops of sky brewing new days
from the fresh grounds of last night.

Remember some people
require more light than others
so make extra.

Dear Me…

This is you.

Sincerely yours
Me.

Origin

There were always words
even when there was no one there
to teach me what they meant
even when the ones I needed most
bent themselves into hooks that
got caught in my throat.

I wrote down the ones
I couldn't bring myself to say
kept them polished and true
for the someday that is finally here.

I don't mean to dig up the past
just let me clear the cemetery out of my throat
because there are some things
you should know.

You should know
that every word I ever wrote
has been a rehearsal for the now
that is finally upon us.

I don't mean to put up a fuss
about love. I just wonder
is there a plot of land in the territory
of your heart for me? Is there a place
where we can lay our regret
to rest peacefully?

You should know
that as a child I planted drops of
blood into the ground like seeds
hoping I could grow your ghost
and finally have a reason for your
absence.

Where were you?
Who were you too busy *being*
that seeing me was back-burnered
for so long that I eventually caught fire

that I became a spire of flame
you were too scared to reach out
to for fear of being burned?

        In your absence
I learned a recipe for an inferno
that turned everything it touched into
ashes that refused to fall apart.

Others called it stubbornness
I called it conviction.

I rubbed words together understanding that
friction was the ingredient needed for the
ember that would grow the blaze in my chest.
I pressed my hands into the world and wondered
if the mark I left would be big enough for
you to finally notice me.

We both made broken into a work of art
we could not bring ourselves to look upon
because we helped sculpt it.

You gave me half this heart but I'm
the one who learned how to make it love.
I'm the one attempting to shove my way
to the front row to the concert of your apology
just to leave a note at your feet that says
you don't have to be sorry.

        All I want
is to know your side of my story.
Give me my origin.

Because up until now it's been lost
in the fire I became anytime anyone
ever asked where my name came from.

When you tell them you don't know
the conversations go from hello to
                                                            goodbye
in the time it takes to make an excuse

good enough to make walking away easy.

You should know
that existence has historically
not been my favourite activity.
It has not been my best subject.
The things your absence made me feel
became three dots I learned to connect
out of order.

So let's start with the second.

The second thing I ever felt was ugly
the first thing I ever felt was unwanted
the third thing I ever felt
was haunted by the belief that
the first thing I felt
was a belt around my neck
that would never loosen
that the gruesome solitude of the hush
between us would leave me hanging
from this breaking branch of our family tree.

Tell me
how many graveyards
make up the acreage
of skeletons in our closet
and I'll tell you how words have
become the composite artist
I use while trying to draw a face for
the missing person of our relationship.

Tell me
that the beginning of us
is not the end of the world
that the python curled around
your voice is dying.

Tell me
that the words in you have
been trying to escape for decades
and that there are parades of noise

ready to march through the quiet
that sprouted up between us
like a mountain neither one of us
believed we could climb.

Tell me
we can recycle clocks
and stop wasting time.

I'm done with the heartbreak of us.

I've read the world
and there are parts that make me smile
chapters like a sundial that can tell time at night
there are stories born in the dark who grow up
knowing they have to make their own light
magicians who practice slight of heart
so no one will know which life their love is in.

It's right here.
I know I'm not supposed to tell
but do you wanna know how I did it?

I hid it in the words
we haven't said to one another yet
laid it evenly across the alphabet
so that each letter could support the
long heavy wait we've both been ready
to let go of for the better part of ages.

I carved it into the pages I wear like skin
wrote hope across my body hoping
it would hold all my red ink in.

When there was no one
there were words.

Words to plug the holes in my sinking suspicion
that blame would only ever offer to sink us
rather than keep us afloat.

There were words that wrote themselves
into rescue boats looking for survivors
amid the wreckage of our story.

Words became the diamonds I mined
from a quarry of depression so
fathomless a sea monster
has been said to live in it.

I know I shouldn't swim there
but I find things in its depth.

I have found music
in the way others volunteer
to complete the unfinished
architecture of my heart
kindness in the shine that
radiates from those who taught me
to chart my escape from darkness
bravery in a kiss laid upon me like
grace stumbling into the long fall of love
virtue in the kind of friendships
that risk sailing with me in these waters.

I have seen enough of doubt
to know that it becomes the
beast that slaughters trust
and leaves wet shreds of dignity
hanging from its greedy teeth.

I planted gardens beneath my feet
to grow my stride toward you
kept an ocean behind my eyes believing
it could extinguish the flames I've been
wearing and stop us both from burning.

I am learning to reach into the dying
womb of ugliness and pull beauty from the
mausoleum it's been trying to become.

        Sometimes
I find rescue in my own hands.

Sometimes
the pen moves as if the commands I give it
sound more like *please*
like I am begging words to assume the shape
of a love I cannot use them to explain.

They do their best.

Growing up without you the
machinery in my chest rusted out
like a storm drain beneath a sky that
would not stop raining.

So here I am
chaining lightning to my thunder
and standing under our family tree
hoping I can salvage your pulse
with my electricity.

When there was no one
(and there was often no one)
there were words.

But none of them will ever echo
as violently as the ones left unspoken
none of them will ever shake our hearts to broken
quicker than the ones we never say.

So I made words my friends
hoping that if I got to know them well enough
they would help me change our story.

I'm sorry I can't rewrite our beginning
but there are better endings to be had.

Growing up
I learned to love words

I'm told my first word was *dad*.

Visiting Hours

During visiting hours
I had to read to sick people
the kind of people who had no one.

It was my punishment—
Catholic school community service
for farting on a nun's muffin
          (it was an accident I swear to god)
and every day would start the same way.

She'd say
    how you doing?
I'd say
          I'm doing alright
she'd say
    I'm doing just fine.

Point in fact the cancer
had taken both of her breasts
and I imagine wherever cancerous breasts
get thrown two of them mourned
their lost body.

She could laugh—
she had a laugh like a welcome mat
wore the same kind of smile
Curious George would wear
if he finally came out of the closet
to be with the man in the big yellow hat.

She'd touch where they used to be
and say
    you know it's probably good that
    they're gone my ex-husband used
    to go about them all wrong.

She'd say
    half the time the only reason my nipples
    were erect was because they were trying

to jump off of my body to run away
from his tongue.

I was thirteen years young
thinking to myself
oh my god you're awesome.

For me it was all about visiting hours.
I hadn't read to her in days
she was too busy teaching me
how to watch horror movies and laugh
because all the monsters Hollywood can think up
just aren't as scary as letting yourself be talked into
believing you can be only half of what you are.

She'd put a hand on each scar
and say
if you really want to get scared
watch the news.

It's a steeplechase—
every day thousands of people face
going under thousands of knives
but it's still more cost-effective
for doctors to pay off lawsuits
than it is to save lives.

So don't try walking a mile in
my shoes just wear my pyjamas
and walk in my dreams instead
because this isn't a deathbed
she'd say
I'm not gonna give up today
I'm not gonna lay here and take it
because life is as elusive as
getting an orgasm from my ex
so sometimes I just got to fake it
so if anyone ever tells you
you're not good enough
you're not smart enough
give up your foolish dream
if anyone ever tells you to quit

you got to make them wear a diaper
on their mouth because man
they are just talking shit

then she'd smile
and say
you've gotta let your body
be the rocking chair
that soothes the tired body of hope
let your arms be the rope around
the neck of self-loathing let
your skin be the clothing
that keeps compassion warm
on the cold streets of regret.

she'd say
don't pray for me yet.

I said
no problem
religion is something
I gave up on along with
dieting but love—
love is a feeling that in
me and through me
I have often called god
so I will love you.

she looked me straight in the heart
and said
it's a shame
they don't make hospital
beds for two but kid you
got your own shit to do
and I can't continue
to let you be doing alright
or be doing just fine not when
there's a world full of people
tired of dressing in shadows
just waiting for you to shine
now bring me my goddamn Jello.

She liked Jello.
She liked me too.

During visiting hours
I had to read to the people
who had no one.

But this is about a woman named everyone.

This isn't about death it's about the fact
that I can still feel her breath in my ear.
Sometimes I can even hear
her say
you are not giving up today.

Because I live in a world
full of seeing-eye underdogs
and I'm pretty sure we're all
tired of wearing our choke chains.
We're tired of being treated like walking
canes in a world so blind no one
can find each other we just
keep bumping into one another
like people are just buildings made of bone
who collapse every time they're made to believe
they were meant to stand
alone.

But you're not.

Some of us can love.

Some of us look like jokes
(not funny)
it's just the way people keep falling for us.

And yeah some of us are going to get cancer
and some of us are going to fall in our
showers but until then you gotta shine
because all the time you get—

it’s just
visiting hours.

For Instance

Take, for instance, you.
Take, for instance, me.
Take, for instance, the fact
that we were getting into
trouble every other
minute…

Like the night you thought it would be cool
to throw a chocolate bar into a hotel
swimming pool then point at it
and yell *shit!*

You said it was something you saw in a movie.
No surprise everyone in that pool was out
instantly.

And we accepted our lifetime ban from the hotel like men
then rolled across town and checked into another
where you proceeded to flirt with a single
mother who was away on a
business trip.

Despite your best efforts later
that day she snubbed you
and you accepted it like
forced retirement.

Take, for instance, the day we spent the night
like millionaires needing to go bankrupt
by sunrise.

Take, for instance, the lies we told our parents
like, *no that is not my sheet of LSD*
I'm holding it for a friend.

Take, for instance, the time you
told me a heart can't break
it can only bend.

Take, for instance, you.

Take, for instance, me.
Take, for instance, the word *instantly*
and how it used to be used to define things like mashed
potatoes or coffee but now somehow they use it
to sum up your life telling
me that you died
instantly.

They said it as if there was a measure of comfort
in the fact that you were dead
that you said no long goodbyes or last words
just gone
like a deadbeat dad who popped
out for some cigarettes and
didn't come back.

Fact is, you were a different kind of gone altogether.
Gone like the promises of lovers who believe
in things like unicorns and forever.

Gone as in never coming back.

Gone as in your parents can't even bring
themselves to go into your old room.

You were gone like that.

But they all said you died instantly.
They said it as if in you was the grace
to not linger like a tragedy in slow motion
or a heartbreak set on pause
no slow cause of death for
us all to deal with.

They said it as if it was a relief
as if that's what you would
have wanted.

And I have seen machines push life into the bodies
of people who would rather just go
and I know that's not something
you would want.

And I'm not saying that I knew you better than most
but I'm pretty sure you'd rather
be alive.

Like the night we decided to drive to the observatory.
We camped under the stars and got drunk.
One beer in you sank into nostalgia
like a love seat tailor-made for
your body.

Listed from memory the top twenty girls
you never kissed but always wanted to
backwards nonstop twenty
through two.

You stopped at number one and said
her name as if once upon a time
you almost did.

We were alive that night.
We watched the dark bleed into twilight watched
the sunrise write novels on the backs of shiny black beetles
and blades of grass.

We read the day cover to cover in one sitting
cloud splitting like lovers lost in a shuffle
of trust and jealousy.

We read our favorite lines out loud.

Yours was:
if my father is ever proud of me
it will mean that in some small measure
I have lived better than him.

Mine was:
if my life is the whim of a dreamer
let them awake and remember
the grand idea that I am
the world's.

Was:

let them stem from me
let them be picked and pressed into diaries
let them be the tangible memories
of writers who could not scribe fictions greater
then those based on the true story of their histories.

Of course, the world didn't actually say that.
We were really high and for once
there was no because to the why.

We spoke like liars finally speaking truth
each word a confessional booth
where we recounted our sins
realizing that the failures of our youth
are what make up the beauty of our
age and every page turned
cannot be rewritten
only reread.

That every chapter we sped through needs
to remain unedited exposing our screw
ups like slips of the nipple
on the evening news.

We were never perfect and
we were only ever
barely amazing.

But I've been thinking about the word *instantly*
and how you lived
instant to instant.

Take, for instance, the night we met
when you wiped the rain out of
your face like sweat and said
it's not raining
it's just the weather
trying to look busy.

We decided right then and there that
the inventor of the umbrella
was a pussy.

Three days later you were sick in bed
reconsidered your position then
called me and said maybe
he was just wise.

My heart is bending.

I keep rereading the ending of your life
expecting the next chapter.
I expect laughter as if
it was always there.

I unexpect your death so hard
that part of me believes
I can make it not true.

You kept a rock on a satin pillow
on your bookshelf and told me
it was a star.

You said you found it in a junkyard and
it had been broken down for quite
some time because too many
people wished on it and
that's a lot of pressure
for one little star.

You are the smile I have kept secret the
Atari eight-bit hero of my youth and
at the funeral your friends all
looked at me as if to say
you're the writer.

So what?

I knew him only as well as he knew me
and when you told me he was gone
I missed him

instantly.

Graffiti

There are stars
now long gone who threw
their last spears of light
across an unending darkness.

But to us
they will ever only be
the stars we see our entire lives.

They will never extinguish.

If you ever need a reminder of the definition of
I don't know

consider that some of the light we see
comes from sources that vanished
eons ago.

Which means maybe everything
is still exploding.

I don't know.

Our questions are tough pills to swallow
(not exactly chewable vitamins)
and yet the confidence in our uncertainty
somehow gives us permission
to hold one another's sins
to each other's noses
like a puppy held to their own shit
like a child's arm to a cigarette.

We turn regret into a hobby
doubt into a pastime
all of this while the winds of change
dodge each chime and the awful
sameness of our pain rings out
like a sound we cannot stop hearing.

Fearing the worst has become
a career option for the brave.

Our leaders save themselves the trouble
of having to care until the graves dug by mental
illness make mercy a platform worth standing on.

Put the heart that goes out to us
back in your chest and start breathing.

You have work to do.

Thoughts and prayers are not enough.

Not when there are razor blades so clever
that they bluff their way past the security
guards of our compassion and cross
some wrists like the finish line for a marathon
we are too tired to keep running.

Not when there are nooses so cunning
that they tangle themselves away
from usefulness and refuse to become
the rope needed to pull us out of this nosedive
we are rehearsing for.

I know what they're for.

But I want to believe that the sleeping pills
scattered on your floor are just dreams
you dropped by accident or the
nightmares you tried to flush.

But I know what they're for.

They're for when love begins to sound like a noise
you cannot bring yourself to listen to any longer.

They're for when you want to unplug the speakers
from the stereo to go as silent as 3:42 am when
the only things still staring back at you

are the stars that might not even
be there anymore.

Some of us run full force toward a closed door
that we come up against like a wall
but others bust through and
fall into a room padded with oblivion
that time then seals shut forever.

We cannot hit rewind on this track.

Your song plays only so long
as you keep singing it
without you we will
not know the lyrics.

I know you are tired of singing.
I know your throat is sore
and your voice raw
from overuse.

I know that tomorrow can feel like
an abuse you are about to suffer.

I know how tempting it can be
to want to put a period on the
end of this incomplete
sentence.

Because is anybody
even reading this?

I don't know.

But maybe there is a paintbrush
that can carve it out better than a blade.

Because the things I've seen made from pain
are works of art that hang in a gallery
displaying sculptures of relief.

Maybe when autumn turns a green leaf yellow
its stem becomes a string tightened to a cello
playing the song you never knew you loved most.

Maybe somewhere there is a ghost
wearing silk sheets hoping to haunt the living
a little more softly.

Maybe somewhere there is someone
who will love you better.

I don't know.

I'm not certain of any of this
but at times I take comfort in leaning
on the shoulder of
I don't know.

To rest against the splendour it provides.

It promises what could be
never what will be.

I don't know if peace
is a talented enough hound
to track down any of us—

but it could be.

I don't know.

Our lives are labyrinths
and I'm lost too.

I dance through its dungeons.
I stumble through its halls.

I vanish while I cry the invisible ink
I use to write my mind
upon its walls.

Instructions For A Bad Day

there will be bad days

be calm
loosen your grip
opening each palm slowly

now let go

be confident
know that now is only a moment
and if today is as bad as it gets
understand that by tomorrow
today will have ended

be gracious
accept each extended hand
offered to pull you back
from the somewhere that
you cannot escape

be diligent
scrape the grey sky clean
realize that every dark cloud
is a smokescreen meant to blind us
from the truth
and the truth is
whether we see them or not
the sun and moon are still there
and always there is light

be forthright
despite your instinct to say
it's alright I'm okay

be honest
say how you feel
without fear or guilt
without remorse or complexity

be lucid in your explanation
be sterling in your repose

if you think for one second no one knows
what you've been going through be
accepting of the fact that you are wrong
that the long drawn and heavy breaths
of despair have at times been felt by everyone
that pain is a part of the human
condition and that alone
makes you legion

we hungry underdogs
we risers with dawn
we dismissers of odds
we pressers of on
we will station ourselves to the calm
we will hold ourselves to the steady

be ready
player one

life is going to come at you armed
with hard times and tough choices
your voice is your weapon
your thoughts ammunition
there are no free extra men

be aware
that in the instant now passes
it exists now as then
so be a mirror reflecting yourself back
and remembering the times when
you thought all of this was too hard and
that you'd never make it through

remember the times
you could have pressed quit
but you hit continue

be forgiving
living with the burden of anger

is not living
giving your focus to wrath
will leave your entire self
absent of what you need
love and hate are beasts
and the one that grows
is the one you feed

be persistent
be the weed growing through
the cracks in the cement
beautiful because it doesn't know
it's not supposed to grow there

be resolute
declare what you accept as true
in a way that envisions the resolve
with which you accept it
if you are having a good day

be considerate
a simple smile could be the first aid kit
that someone has been looking for
if you believe with absolute honesty
that you're doing everything you can
take a breath

now do more

there will be bad days
times when the world weighs on you for so long
it leaves you looking for an easy way out

there will be moments when the drought of joy
seems unending instances spent pretending
that everything's alright when it so clearly is not

check your blind spot

see that love is still there
every nightmare has a beginning
but every bad day has an end

ignore what others have called you
I'm calling you friend

everyone knows pain
but we are not meant to carry it forever
we were never meant to hold it so closely

so be certain in the belief that
what pain belongs to now
will belong soon to then
that when someone asks you
how was your day
realize that for some of us
it's the only way we know how to say

be calm
loosen your grip
opening each palm slowly

now let go

I Like You Too

There is a gravity in you so heavy
it begs me to wonder if other hands
have experienced the same difficulty as mine.

When my hands set down
on the spaces you allow them
they feel compelled to never leave.

There are magnets in
the way I feel about you
like there is fruit in the Jello.

I like you too.
I like you *sooo* too.

I like that you keep your shoulder blades
sharp enough to cut through the maybe knots
that have kept me tangled up in hesitation like
a marionette practicing bondage.

My spine is the bridge where my
heart meditates on the difference
between diving and falling.

My pulse is the busy signal gravity gets
when calling to collect payment for
keeping my feet on the ground.

Because the butterflies in my stomach
were just caterpillars before they met you.

They did not begin rehearsing flight
until they were sure you were the sky.

I like you too.

My laugh has been the overdue library book
that I thought would never be returned
believed all the pages had been torn
out and burned to warm someone else's

lonely nights but you bring back my smile
like you bring back hardcore to pillow fights.

On the list of things I like
you rank above cowboys walking wiener dogs
                    and cowboys walking wiener dogs
                                        ranks very very high.

And yet you are somehow above it.
You make me admit to joy.
You make me confess to the I love it.

I am as guilty of happiness
as I am innocent of despair.

You are the never-ending music that
invites me to dance around the electric chair
that's been begging me to take a seat.

You are the cheat code that makes me run faster
jump farther walk through walls and breathe fire
and when it feels as though I'm stuck
you slip chains around each tire to remind me
that sometimes we have to dig into the dirt
and make the path bend to the direction we choose.

To live like we lost our nothing-to-lose back
when we were still wondering if our everything-to-gain
would be enough to explain why we risked it all
to carve scars in the shape of one another
back into each other like initials into trees.

So please understand that when I say
I like you too
I'm not just echoing words back to you.

I am celebrating the fact that you said
these words to me at all because I can't recall
a time when it didn't feel like my best
guess was just another wrong
answer waiting to happen.

When I asked you what word you liked
you said *context*
because it changes everything.

So let me bring you these long stem possibilities
none of them written in stone just sewn
into whatever vase you provide
whatever context you put them in.

Because I've been watching the way
sunflowers blush in moonlight
and it reminds me of the radiance you
use to slay my shadows of doubt.

You shout into my silence like an
orchestra detonating requiems in my sleep.
You steep yourself like tea into this broken cup
I keep locked behind a cabinet of bones
ribs like thin tombstones marking a resting place
for something I could swear I once buried there.

I didn't count on you becoming the skeleton key
that would open up these parts of me
didn't think anyone would want to unearth
the silly string and crazy glue
but I grab the shovel and dig up
these parts of me for you

because I like you too.

I like that you splash around in
the puddle of me and turn
my stillness into chaos.

You cross my mind like
an ambulance crossing a city
all other considerations clear a path
and stop to make way for the thought of you.

I like you so too it feels
like an emergency.

Like we are riding in the back of a flashing red comet
etching ourselves into the universe like a scratch of light
against the smooth black finish of a night so never ending
all we can do is claw at it with our own shine.

I like you
is the headline I want thrown
against my doorstep every morning
front page in big bold letters like a warning
that no other news is as important
as this small declaration of war
against loneliness.

In this battle for joy we are
not often sent reinforcements.

Self-doubt prints propaganda
that says if we surrender we will not
be fired upon but your presence in my life
is the weapon I keep drawn against
the oncoming bayonets of that lie.

So make my aim true
because I like that you like
the way I like you.

And I love that you
like me like that
too.

Fish

Not that you ever do…

but if you ever wonder
your friendship is a hook

that you cast into an ocean
where I practice drowning.

Your love is a lure so brilliant
that it makes me bite into the pain.

You make the hurt worth enduring.

You bring me to the surface and my gills blossom
like flowers surrendering to new atmosphere.

If it looks like I'm trying to breathe it's because
I'm suffocating on the oxygen you provide.

A yawn can look like a scream
with the volume turned down.

So let my choking on this air look like laughter
because you sure make it feel that way.

You are funny.

Funny like the fact that you have a self-
diagnosed condition that you call back flatulence.

The first time I witnessed it I was struck apart
into laughter by an orgasm of joy so ferocious

it must have looked like a care bear
after being gassed up at the dentist's office.

You are funny like the fact that you add
your own sound effects to the world around you.

When the click of a button is not enough
you add *boink*.

I do my best not to wonder what mystifying carnival
of noises your lovers must walk through

what perplexing squeals make up
the bouquet of your intimacies.

You are funny like the fact that you
thought Vegas would be a good idea

to go partying amid the never-ending
onslaught of blinking lights.

Despite the fact that
you have epilepsy.

Funny as hell.

But if I ever lost you that way or any other
I would feel the departure of your gravity in my life.

I would feel the ocean rise up around mountains as if its
hunger was promoted to the head of the starvation department.

You would be as missed
as moonlight.

You would fuck with the tides.

I would be devastated if one day the lure
of you stopped showing up in my ocean.

If the beacon that gives me comfort suddenly
stopped flashing and the darkness of

the water around me thickened into a presence
more difficult to swim through.

Because you are the someone who annoys me
with joy until I wave a white flag to it.

You are the reservoir I draw from
when life requires strength.

Which is just a little over all the time.

You accept the weirdness in me like
I am giving you a snow globe.

You don't know where the fuck you're going to put it but
you know that I have been put in junk drawers before.

You know that I have been neighbours with broken
pens and orphaned beams of staples

that want nothing more than to keep it together
whatever it happens to be.

So you make space for me in your life.

You keep me on display
at your kitchen table.

Granted I am still surrounded by junk but we often hold
strange communion there in the heart of your peculiar palace.

We play racquetball with ideas and we do not go easy
even on the nights your back flatulence is acting up.

We get right into the bruises of it.

We open the wound as if unpacking a delicacy and
we go through it together learning to eat

our pain with these strange utensils
we call hearts.

There are parts of us that even the greedy
hands of clocks cannot touch.

Even the circadian nature of decay can
only serve to amplify its shine.

My memories of you are stored in the
cellar of my attic like a vintage wine.

Old quilts of fine dust camouflage the gleam beneath
but a light wipe polishes away the time and

the glass begins to look like a jewel
I cannot bring myself to part with.

You are priceless.

The fangs of temptation will be stopped at
the gates of how much you mean to me.

I will never gamble with
the ruby in your chest.

You are my friend.

You are valued so far beyond appraisal that the concept
of any other kind of wealth becomes gibberish to me.

And when you hurt I want to touch
the part of you that aches.

Boink.

Because when my despair becomes a leviathan when
the small hooks won't suffice and breath turns to dread

the instant I become a sunken ship
you raise me from ruin.

You cast anchors instead.

Heaven or Whatever

"You can't just do whatever."

The words stumbled out of you like a drunk
leaving a bar looking for a fresh new last call.
You were not a man of words
but did your best to offer advice.
You offered me

"You can't just do whatever."

And I know what you meant.

You meant that whatever I choose to
do I must not be aimless.
I must not just spin the globe
and go wherever I stick my finger
because seventy-one percent of the time
I will end up in the ocean and
if I do end up in the ocean
I can't just do whatever.
I better learn to swim.

"You can't just do whatever."

The conversation came after you asked me about heaven
told me that you thought heaven would be specific
to each person and that each person would
have their own version of it.

Then asked me what would mine be.

And I was so scared to tell you
I don't have one.

But you nodded your head as if confirming a suspicion
that perhaps school had robbed me of a belief in some stories.
You said "You don't have to believe what I believe
it's enough to be good."

Be good.

I will.

I will think about your heaven.

Your heaven would be the same haircut forever
it would be a stick a dog and some distance
a lawn that always needs mowing
a six pack of pilsner short bottles
and your real teeth back because
your dentures could never master
that bottle opening trick
that you loved to do.

The first time you tried it with dentures
I had nightmares for a month because
I thought your mouth had fallen off.

Your heaven would be Austria before the war
and Canada after you met Grandma.

It would be headcheese sandwiches and blood
sausage other deli meats that would ensure
you'd never ever have to entertain dinner guests
and I would never be in danger
of having my lunch stolen.

Your heaven would be a stash of raisins
and problems that you could fix with your hands.

I remember you tried to fix everything
with your hands.

I remember the difficult days.
I remember the bandages.
They looked like blankets as if
your knuckles had all gone off to bed.
Walls that looked like they'd said
something that got under your skin
and were suddenly made to pay for it.

I know you were an angry man.
Fingertips like spent shotgun shells

bleeding smoke cocktails of gunpowder
and singed plastic.

You had what some people would call
"a temper."

But you loved a good joke
even if it was on you.

Something that would crack open the walls
of your chest and let the wind tickle your heart
just enough to let you know it was still there.

You didn't always laugh.
You didn't always smile.

You did keep a mental ledger of what
you called your "send flowers list."

I remember thinking it was a thank you to
those who got you good but learned the truth
after my grandma added a thin layer of sand to
your sandwiches because you refused to
make your own lunch for work.

You told me about it when you picked
me up from school that day.
You said Grandma just made the "send flowers list"
and I asked "because you love her so much?"
and you said "because I'm gonna kill her."

Of course you didn't.

Your version of kill meant two months before winter
having a seamstress take in each of her coats in
a few inches so on the first day she needed one
she fumbled with the sudden tightness
and you stood there smiling then
said in between laughs
"Honey I love you no matter how big you get."

She did not laugh
and managed to staple your
smile back into a straight face
when she told your friends at work
that she had to move into the spare room
because you couldn't stop farting at night.

You often asked me *if*...

If I had a heaven what would it be like?

And I told you that for such a small word
if
is just too big to wrap my belief around.

I would not bend to the hypothetical
but wish now that I would have
even if it was just to ease your mind
in the belief that I could be headed
to that other place you believed in.

I would tell you now how
my heaven is here.

It was here in the gentle warfare
of your relationship with Grandma
where volleys were traded back and forth
like hockey cards between children
who didn't care what the stats meant.

My heaven would have been someone in grade five
finally willing to trade me their fruit roll up
for my tin of sardines.

My hell was wondering why.

Why would you give me
sardines for lunch?

My heaven would make you laugh
because I get the feeling that
you didn't get to do that very much.

Through my hell
through the night terrors
and bloody noses
through the eyes black
bruised back
sneak attack
knapsack and winter coat highjacks
you did your best to seal up the cracks
in my armor and made
my heaven here.

I would have loved to have made you laugh more
to make your "send flowers list" just once.

So I offer you now my *if*…

If there is a heaven
mine would have a post office
so I could send letters to yours.

The first letter would read
"Hell's not so bad.
They pretty much
let you do whatever."

When I Was A Kid

when i was a kid
i hid my heart under the bed
because my mother said
if you're not careful
someday someone's
gonna break it

take it from me under the bed
is not a good hiding spot

i know because i've been shot down
so many times i get altitude sickness
just from standing up for myself

When i was a kid i could fill a bookshelf
with every different way they
would tell me how not to play

they'd say
    it's time to start putting childish things away
and i was like
    fuck you
    this is skeletor

but more and more they made me
believe our hearts are like door knocks
and that's where we get the beat
and i'll never get to meet the man
inside me if i can't stand still
long enough to be there
i'll never make it anywhere
if i just keep running away
i'll never know myself
if all i ever do is play
nicky nicky nine doors

they asked
    don't you want to be a man?

and when I was a kid
i wanted to be a man

i wanted a registered
retirement savings plan
that would keep me in candy
long enough to make old age sweet
i wanted two left feet
so that i could dance in circles
around important issues
until way past my bedtime

i'm not saying that i don't have opinions
just that others were less likely to argue
if they were as tired as i was

fatigue does to men what
a goodnight kiss does to kids
it puts weights on our eyelids
and returns us to a place
where reason and imagination
lace together shoes whose
tongues stick out at stillness
and beckon us to move forward.

as a kid i was always drawn toward moonlight
despite an armada of adults who insisted
i must set my days according to sunlight
i would lay in bed and fight sleep
believing that if i shut my eyes
even for an instant i would miss
out on something amazing

turns out i was right

i have seen stars stamped into the
nightlike cookie cutter designs
i drew lines between each one
and played connect the dots
i invented new constellations
so that when people asked me
    what's your sign

i could point to mine
the one hanging over the first
door past the finish line
and say
    it's right there
    the one marked exit

because one day all this getting
ahead bullshit will be over
and people will start looking for
me and i'll be there
i'll wear my best flashing
red and you

you will stand
winners circle thoroughbred
i will unthread the screws that were
put to you throughout this life
then smile and say
    you made it

when i was a kid i traded in homework
assignments for friendship
then gave each friend a late slip
for never showing up on time
and in most cases not at all
i gave myself a hall pass
to get through each broken promise

and i remember this plan born out of frustration
from a kid who kept calling me yogi
then pointed to my tummy and
said too many picnic baskets

it's not that hard to trick a dumb ass

one day before class i said
    yes you can copy my homework
and gave him all the wrong answers
that i'd written down the night before

he got his paper back expecting a near
perfect score and couldn't believe it
when he looked across the room at me
and held up a zero

i know i didn't have to hold up my paper
of twenty-eight out of thirty but my satisfaction
was complete when he looked at me
puzzled and i thought to myself
smarter than the average bear motherfucker

when i was a kid i slid love letters
through the slots of lockers
that belonged to my secret crushes
built paint brushes from the tiny
hairs that stood on end every time
i saw them my brain stem finally
blooming into thoughts

i connected dots and made
masterpieces each brushstroke a thesis
dedicated to the explanation that you
not knowing who i was
was only because anonymity
made it easier to be brave

i dipped my brush into a tidal wave of
i hope this will one day wash over me

i can guarantee if you've ever had a secret
admirer it was someone very much like me
who loved someone very much like you

it was someone who wanted to tell you
how much you've meant how
every second we spent thinking of you
was simply the cost of getting us through
the hard times

we saved nickels and dimes
hoping our first date would be with you

through the discipline of love we gave
up on candy bars and video games

i promise you that every guy i've ever met
remembers the names of the ones they loved first
that our thirst for love continues as we cross the deserts
of maybe believing that we will find an oasis of
    yes we acquiesce

yes we probably should have just said
something but we were chickenshit
we lit the fuses to our hearts and
exploded every time
you walked on by

when I was a kid I did stupid shit
ripped the women's underwear section
out of the sears christmas wish catalogue
and then blamed it on my granddad

he did end up covering for me
and had only this to say
    you're only twelve so i'm impressed
    but take it from experience don't
    hide that shit under your mattress

so i didn't

i hid it in the empty box of a board game
that i never used to play and on the day
when my grandmother eventually found it
she reamed him out for hiding pornography
in her grandson's bedroom

the impending doom of the truth
set upon me like a dying sun sending its
last ray of light over the horizon
and aimed directly at me

he didn't say a word
incurred the full wrath
and laughed with me later saying

it's like your heart
it doesn't matter
where you hide it

lovers are like little kids lifting up
a rock looking for an insect

they *will* find that shit

when i was a kid i trusted myself enough
to know that one day i would be a man
one day i'd have a childhood for a past
and a future for a back-up plan
that every gauntlet I ever ran
was a potato sack race in which
time would chase me further toward
an ending

i am bending myself back to the beginning
reminding myself there is no winning any
race against yourself

slow down

and when the kid in you falls
turn around pick them up dust them
off and then continue

trust me
you are going to need that kid

you are going to need someone to remind you
that every weed is a flower just trying to make
shit work that every jerk you ever encounter
is just another someone who somehow forgot
it's okay to need a hug
it's okay to be afraid

as a kid i played hopscotch
with the lines they drew in the sand
landed on the conclusions that second-hand clothes
at least had the benefit of experience

and i've got a 137th-hand heart
broken apart and stitched back
together at the seams

i've cartwheeled across balance
beams made from the broken finger bones
of people who could not let go of this life

i still love the night
i love the fact that if you squint
your eyes just right stars look like
porcupines of white stumbling across the
dark dipping their quills into the night
trying to write apologies for all of the
unanswered wishes from the times
we once wished upon them
and sometimes i still wish
and most times i wish
i didn't have to

i wish i never had to wish

so i guess what i'm saying is that
i hope

i hope i never forget that kid
who grew up inside me
he just seemed to laugh a little bit
louder smiled just a little bit longer
loved a whole lot stronger
worlds first official awesome-
monger taking awesome from door
to door
take as much as you need
don't worry about me
i've got more

i've got a candy store filled with whatever
it's gonna take to make tomorrow sweet
i've got two left feet and no bedtime
i'm still not brave enough to have an orgy
but i rock the slumber party

come nap with me
first one to fall asleep loses
first one to fall asleep wins
the race stops at the start
and the finish line is where it begins
so this time first one to lose wins

i know we never meant to turn
our hearts into garbage bins

it was an accident

i know the headlines about us giving up
were a misprint and really
just bad reporting

i know we've been boarding up
all the windows from the outside in
we've been doing it ever since they told
us to start letting things go

and i know we got into the habit
of just throwing things away
but your heart is a door knock
and every time it beats it's
just that kid's way of asking

can you please come out and play?

Crush

I've been thinking about the word crush
and how you were my first
and how the worst thing that
could have happened
happened.

When you and I were ten
we were made to work together on a
grade five presentation about animals.

I was so nervous.

Without ever having known you
I would reminisce about how
you fell in love with me.

It was your typical love story—
school is attacked by zombies
and shy kid saves the day.

I think about the way I was when I was younger
about how my hunger for acceptance drove
me to cannibalize my fantasies of love
into loneliness believing everyone
else would have to die just
for you to love me.

But in a role reversal I never expected
you fingertip-drew halos around
the heads of snow angels.

You saved me.

Alone together in the back of a library
we studied each animal's secret society
and learned the use of the collective noun.

Example:
  a murder of crows.

God knows it sounds ominous
but this is how I learned about community.
We have names for the groupings that
occur even in the open ocean:
    a battery of barracuda
    a shiver of sharks
    a school of fish.

And I pondered the philosophy that since barracudas
and sharks are technically fish wouldn't the term
school of fish encapsulate them as well?

It wasn't long before you went on to tell me that
each term was in some way meant to suggest
the nature of each beast:
    a destruction of wildcats
    a crash of rhinoceroses.

This is not meant to say that each animal
is considered in some way deadly.
There are those who sound
downright lovely:
    a murmuration of starlings
    a kindle of kittens
    an exaltation of larks.

some are meant to sound industrious or prestigious:
    a parliament of owls
    a labour of moles.

but I feel for the outcasts:
    a smack of jellyfish
    an implausibility of wildebeest
    an apology of Canadians.

You loved the classification:
    a cowardice of curs.

Believed that this is where the term underdog
stems from that sometimes we become more
than the definitions that are thrust upon us
that we can bite back that

a pack of wolves
is part of our ancestry and in the
moment we embrace our history
we become a new destiny
we can rewrite a legacy
because we are
a storytelling of ravens.

I began applying this concept to my life
arriving at the conclusion that dickheads
congregate in groups and I cannot
describe the solemn pride that was mine
when I was sent home with a report
card and a statement written by
my hard-ass gym teacher that read
Shane does not work well in groups.

I told this to you and we both laughed and
maybe it was my happiness that gave me away
betrayed my position to the three boys
who'd made a hobby out of
making me cry.

I still remember the impact from when
they pushed me over in my chair and you—
you could have just sat there.
I wouldn't have been angry.
But instead you decided to teach me that assholes—
assholes come in bunches.

I learned this fact in the back of that library.
You helped me up off the ground
then turned around to tell my attackers
you guys are
a bunch of assholes

We were ten.

If you ever want to know how it feels to
be saved just let someone save you
let someone rescue the smile
drowning inside you.

It's not too late I swear.

See I once hid my heart in a hat and pulled out
a rabbit that ran away just so I could say
it was a vanishing act
    ta da!
But through you I learned that real
magic is about making things
come back.

I know because when a ten-year-old girl
can go on to shock three bullies into silence
you know that you have just determined
your lifelong definition of beautiful
and all the other wonderful instances
in your existence will volunteer
to dim their brilliance so that
throughout your life this moment
will shine brightest.

You made the best snow angels.

Laid them out in threes
like paper dolls holding hands.
You laid them side by side and said it was because
even two people can feel alone.

I think of the time I would have destroyed
the world just so I could be with you.

I've grown up since then
but think often of a time when
I placed a penny on top of a penny
on top of a railroad track and then waited
for a train to squish one coin into the other
so I could give you a two-cent piece
because you were scared that someday
they'd raise the price of one-cent candies.

These are the ways I loved you.

You were the only one to give me a valentines day card
granted you gave one to everyone but hard to
believe that you gave the best one to me.
The other boys were jealous of a small card
with a picture of a shark biting a heart and saying
    I think you're jawsome.

Wanted to draw you a card of a
crab pinching a heart saying
    I think you're crabulous.

My granddad advised me against it
citing that in my teens I would understand
why that's not a good idea.

And now every time I see a lone snow angel
I think of you.

So I offer you now
    a crush of hearts
    a sacrifice of body parts
laid upon the altar of better times
when the lines inside of a coloring
book were only suggestions.

Girl sometimes you gotta scribble
gotta color the sun purple
just so you know what it feels
like to be in charge sometimes you
gotta love just a little so you can
finally start to live large.

I offer you
    a lifetime of held breaths
    a juggernaut of thank-you's
    a thimble of blues
and
    a who's who of I-miss-you's.

Because I am made up of memories
and these ones are the diamonds
I have kept polished

just so I know what it feels like
to treasure something.

I've been thinking about the word crush
and how you were my first
and how the worst thing that
could have happened
happened.

When you turned eleven and moved away
didn't even get to say goodbye because
you moved in the summer and I
returned to a school where your absence
echoed in my ears for all of the years
I had left to deal with what it
feels like to be alone.

I've grown up since then
but think often of the time when
we were ten when you made snow angels
hold hands laid them down side by side and I
tied my definition of beauty
to your memory.

We never even kissed
because you probably never knew.

But goddamn—
I had the biggest crush on you.

How to be a person

1. Find your voice.

    Know that not all languages contain words.
    Your voice could be music it could be dance.
    It will be what expresses you most sincerely.

    Your voice is an art.
    If your heart is broken make art with the pieces.

2. Remember that you are an artist regardless
    of how constantly the world will try to drive
    it out of you or how a "real job" will try to
    bury the part of you that communicates your
    feelings when language fails.

    You are an artist
    whether it is with food or building robots.
    You will know your medium
    the instant you realize how in love
    you are with what it brings out of you.

3. Apologize.

    You will not always be right.
    You will not always be wrong.
    You will (hopefully) always be learning.
    Atonement is a sacrifice of pride.
    Explanation of why you did what
    you did or said what you said
    will not vindicate you.

    If the cost to heal someone is only your pride
    then apologize and be grateful that you
    received peace at such a bargain.

4. Forgive.

    Realize that some people are still learning.
    If forgiveness is not possible then think

of everything you ever wanted to be
forgiven for but weren't.

Hold that uneasiness in your mind
until you feel your desire for absolution
becoming a wish.
Realize you can grant this wish for others.

If you are waiting for forgiveness
be prepared to wait.
Be prepared to stand in the path of time
and wither respect that forgiveness is difficult.
Not all trespasses are equal and not everyone
will heal according to your schedule.

5. Accept that farting is funny.
Granted—
not always appropriate
and sometimes unpleasant.

But if you cannot laugh—
if you are more offended by a fart
than by war, famine, political corruption, deforestation
racism, sexism, classism, the wrongfully imprisoned,
the treatment of women, the foreclosing on homes
while banks debts are forgiven—
if a fart offends you more than any of that—
then you are not a person
and cannot be helped.

Join a cult and drink the Kool-Aid.

6. Know that love is a vulnerability
but not a weakness.

Love is the volunteer in you that raises its
hand and steps forward without needing
to be rewarded.

Love is a currency that functions in reverse
because the only way to be wealthy with it
is to give more of it away.

7. Don't laugh to fit in.

   Laughter should be honest.
   If there is no sincerity in your joy
   then your happiness will be a forgery
   that fools only yourself.

8. Do not fear to be hated but be
   cautious towards those inhabited by hate.

   You will be hated regardless of
   who you are what you say
   or what you do.

   You will be hated for your successes
   or your failures for good looks or bad looks
   for intelligence or stupidity.

   Hate is the child of the hater
   nurtured by the beliefs it is fed.

   You often will have no control
   over what you are hated for.
   Know that antipathy becomes
   the master of its owner.
   Know that if you are going to be hated
   regardless of who you are then be
   fearless enough to be who you want to be.

   Hate is no more eloquently articulated
   than in the poetry of the expression
   not your fucking problem.

9. Try.

   The tiniest dream that you try to make happen
   is worth more than the biggest dream
   you never attempt.

10. Be savagely thankful and continuously in awe
    of the power you possess.

You are alive inside of an endless cosmos
with a freedom that shines brightest in the dark.

Choices
your choices
belong to you so intimately
that they will never leave you.

They
unlike the changing nature of love
or the failing machinery of our bodies
will never abandon you to time
good or bad.

They will stay always an antique
that shows the future who you were
and what you stood for.

Know that what you choose to stand for is
what will inform you of what you've chosen
to stand against.

So stand.

Let each foot crash land into what you
believe and plant them their firmly
so they may take root in your convictions.

And stand.

For Many

The question has been posed to many:

If you could change anything about
your body what would it be?

Me?

I'd change my nose.

I'd turn it into a rose so that every
time you leaned in to smell it
I could steal kisses.

I know this is not what you had in mind
that you were only trying to find some
simple thing about me that I would change
as if my body were a rack of Scrabble tiles that
I could rearrange and exchange for better letters
because it seems the world has got us all
trying to spell *beauty*

So here we sit.

Shearing metal sheep for the steel wool
that we will use to scrub away our flaws
hoping each eye of every beholder is an artist
that draws gentler conclusions than the ones
we have about ourselves.
How can we be beautiful in a world
that delves no deeper than our skin?

The question has been asked to many.

So often that wishing wells spit back pennies
sick of the copper poisoning they get from our dreams.
It seems we still think we can buy our desires
for the price of next to nothing.
We've been stuck inside of a mentality
that suggests changing yourself is limited only

to your dimensions as if our bodies are
customizable but our attitudes or beliefs are not.
We behave as if thought is not malleable
as if ideas are inflexible.
We pull the trigger on the question
and expect something simple in response.
We expect nonchalance about the bullet
hole and detachment about the bleeding.
We expect not needing to spend a
second thought thinking about it.
We expect answers to be immediate.

We are expected to have thought about this
our entire lives and now we are being asked
so be quick—

If you could change anything about
your body what would it be?

Me?

I'd change my eyes into your eyes
so that every time I look in the mirror
I could see what it is about me that you
think needs changing.

We've been listening to something
that's only function is to see.
We've been basing beauty on our eyes
the same tool we first learned to judge
with the blacksmith to our prejudice—

too fat too thin
bad teeth worse skin
no chin big nose
small breasts long toes
poor looks cheap clothes
it goes too short too tall
too nothing too all.

The things we call each other in the name
of beauty are ugly in that they allow

no contrast to symmetry as if we want
the grandness of the theatre without the sets
the bad choices without regrets
the bright shiny future without the dark
tragic history.

We forget that muscles don't mean strength of character.
We blur the lines between the two and forget that
pretty does not always mean nice
the same way beautiful doesn't
always mean an easy life.

We live in a world where children
would rather go under the knife
than wait to see who they'll
grow up to be.

The question has been asked to many.

Me?

I'd change my bowels into a remote control
so I could fast forward through this shit
change my chest into a juke box and hit *evolve*
because someone's gotta change this same
old song we've been singing as if
bringing each other down is getting
us anywhere other than
nowhere fast.

We are building a world where people
curse the DNA passed down to them
because when you ask the question

If you could change anything about
your body what would it be?

what you're really asking me is

Is there is some part of myself that I hate?

Great question.
And it has been asked to many.

But we are not Mr. or Mrs. Potato Head
go customize a friend go Photoshop a lover
go put your attitude on the cover of a fashion magazine
and see if anyone calls it beautiful.

You act as if you won't one day be old
as if you won't one day shake your head
at all the product they sold you
promises of vanishing lines
and tighter skin surgeries that do nothing
other than dress up your skeleton
as if there is no longer any grace in getting old
or being who you are.

They stuffed empty promises in a jar
and convinced you
you need this.

Pretty is a lie designed to sell you back to yourself.
But you are still you underneath the biceps or
the great hair underneath everywhere they said
you could hide underneath the color contact
blue-eyed picture of perfection and right down
past the sinew that keeps it all in place.

You are still you.

You are still bound to your own
proclivities and perspectives.
Appearance forgives nothing.
It cannot excuse you from being who
you are and if who you are has not
come far enough to know that
then go stand in line with monotony.

We will still be here
living up to the more intangible
qualities in the definition of beauty.

You asked us:

If we could change anything about
our body what would it be?

For many it goes far beyond bone or skin.

Many would change their minds
into doors and they would
leave them open
to let you in.

Turn On A Light

The three things you really need to
know about my granddad are
number one
and probably most important
he had an intense love
for beef jerky.

Two he had the kind of bad temper
that could be likened to a levy
bursting apart on a hot dry day.
A cache of anger stored away
for any given moment
on any given day.

My mother used to say he was one-half
volcano and one-half hurricane
a handful of excuses and
a gut full of pain.

And because of this we come to
number three.

My granddad had a way with monsters.

As a child I slept in a bedroom
full of them a closet stuffed with
long-legged demons who could make it
from one end of the room to the other
in a single step.

My strep-throat silence was
born from night terrors when
screaming was not enough so I instead
kicked the wall drew my first remembered breath
the moment I heard thunder stomp
down the hall then burst through my door
like a war on its way to a peace protest.

My granddad would rest his hands on his
hips let his fingertips grip his boxers

then lift them up past his waist.
Standing like a superhero in the doorway
he would split the night with a whisper
and say

Alright you motherfuckers
I swear to Christ I will turn on
a goddamn light.

Never has any monster ever heard
a battle cry more terrifying than

I will turn on a light.

And every night
for more than four years
my granddad took boogeymen by
the ears and through them out
on their asses dragged the carcasses
of dead monsters out of my room
grabbed a broom then swept what was
left of my nightmares into a dustpan
emptied them into a trashcan
then turned around to say

Sweet dreams my boy
I'm down the hall if you need me.

We were sidekicks.
I'd sound the alert and my granddad
would put the hurt on whatever was
hiding under my bed or lurking in my closet.
He'd deposit his foot so deep into the asses of gargoyles
that when they finally turned back into stone
he could wear them as platform boots
to a Kiss concert.

My granddad used to wear a red polo shirt to bed.
He said that it used to be white but one night
when I was four he busted down my bedroom door
and had to kick some ass because I was screaming
and now he was wearing it as a warning

teaching nighttime that there are things
far worse than the morning.

A night terror differs from a nightmare
in that the dreamer will awake
and take terror with them
back into consciousness.
Add to this the fact that the dreamer
rarely recalls what they dreamt
and that any attempt to wake them
usually ends unsuccessfully.

I know this now
but think constantly how
my granddad had to just stand
there and wait for it to end.
How the following day he'd
pretend not to be tired an alarm clock
wired into fears I could not recall
he'd wake and thunder down the hall
doing the very best he could.

He'd be there
an anchor pulling me
back from the somewhere
I could not escape.

As a child I learned not every hero wears a cape
not everyone gets a ticker-tape parade
just for having patience.
Not everyone has the confidence
needed to just stand there wait for it to end
and believe everything
is going to be okay.

Not everyone has the strength to say or do
nothing when a child is screaming
dreaming of eternity in a room with no doors
no floors to keep you from falling further into panic
each once small fear suddenly titanic
in its implications situations so far

beyond grotesque I would have amputated
my own imagination just to make them stop.

But at the end of each one
he'd be there and he'd say

Cover your eyes
I'm going to turn on a light.

He'd invite me back to consciousness with a tired smile.
He'd put me back to bed and say

I'll be down the hall if you need me.

The next day he would sit on the
sofa before dinner and say

I just need to rest my eyes.

Rest.

My quest to end night terrors
was born from the night he ended up
falling asleep at the wheel and driving
full speed into a snowbank.

My one man think tank kicked into overdrive
and for five nights in a row my granddad
slept soundly free from worry.
We watched the light return to his eyes
as if it had just come back
from a long vacation.

But on night number six
the kicks against the bedroom wall
made thunderstorms down the hall once more.

He stood in the doorway ready to wage war
ready to restore light to darkness to
dismiss shadows to land heavy-
handed blows Muhammad Ali combos
that would give monsters pause

to reconsider the options—
get up or stay down.

Stay down.

That night he was hungry for a first-round knockout.
He was about to go through his usual checklist
of monster hiding spots when I said

No it's okay
go back to bed.

With renewed enthusiasm he looked at me and said

Nonsense
these assholes have to pay.

I remember the way he dropped to his knees
stuck his head under my bed
and said

what the fuck is all of my beef
jerky doing under here?

I explained to him my not so brilliant plan.
I said

I thought if I kept them fed they'd leave me alone
and you could get a good night's sleep.

Slow but deep his lips crept across his
face and then cracked open into laughter.
After a childhood of expecting only anger
he lay down on the ground his lungs
kicking at his chest every suppressed joy
suddenly brought to the surface.

This is the first time that I can recall
hearing my granddad laugh.

Some thoughts are kept in closets
hanging next to skeletons and boogeymen.

Sometimes when we believe in monsters
they take up residence under our beds
and our heads fill with the dread
needed to keep them fed.

We tend to tread our own fear
because we somehow thought it was
better off being kept secret.

It should come as no surprise that
some hearts are like dark bedrooms
tombs that we allowed ourselves to shut
because we thought that way
everything would be alright.

I think of my granddad's laugh.
I think often about that night about
how some people are waiting for people like us
to slide our hands against their walls
and say

Cover your eyes
we're about to turn on a light.

The Student

I don't believe
in them

but somewhere there are gods
hiding inside of their own heads
using all their might trying to
stop their own eardrums from
pounding out the sound of your name

you are lightning
trying to tame thunder
leaving split second
scars against the sky
as if you were breaking the skin
of something that won't die

my first instinct
is the same as my second
strongly reinforced as if
by a diamond sheeting that
donated its glimmer to charity
so that it could look dull and tough
a shine now scuffed
as if the world left a
bruise on light

I fight my instinct long enough
to realize that I won't win
I give in
surrendering to an impulse
somewhat believing that my
imprisonment will not involve torture
if I confess everything I know

I know
nothing

I bring an emptiness to your need like a dog
laying a skeleton at your feet
bone by bone

I lay stone
all around you in a circle
as if at any moment you will
burst into flame and warm us long enough
so that I can tell you my ghost story

that a part of me still haunts my memory
it throws chairs against my mirrored mind
cracking the reflections in which I
once thought I would find
answers

if I reflect long enough
there will be answers

but like mail on
Sunday none came

so I sit before flowers
hoping they will train
me in the art of
opening up

I stand on mountain tops believing
that avalanches will teach me to let go

I know nothing
but I am here
to learn

Move Pen Move

Stay.

That's what mothers say
when their sons and
daughters go away.

They say
stay.

My mother said
go.

So I wasn't there the night she fell out
of her wheelchair so frustrated that
she amputated her own legs
or rather tried to
her life leaking out onto the
white floor blossoming
like roses in the snow.

Our relationship was an anthem
composed of words like
gotta go.

So we went.

And sent our regards
on postcards from all the places we'd been
with stories about all the things we'd seen.

That's how it was with you and I.
Why say goodbye when
we could still write?

But then it took
your hands.

We should've practiced our goodbyes
because then it
took your eyes.

And I was somewhere
in the middle of nowhere
watching the sun rise over a stop
sign placed down the centre
line of a highway
filled with sudden turns
for the worse running
back home 'cause
I gotta play nurse.

Gotta figure out which pill
alleviates which pain
which part of your
brain is being used for a
boxing bag as your body
became a never-ending game
of freeze tag taking place in an
empty playground.

I was left looking for your
limbs in a lost and found

and I couldn't set
you free.

So we just sat there
our heads bent towards
each other like flowers
in the small hours
of the morning
while light wandered in
like a warning that time is passing
and you right along with it.

Bit by bit
every day.

And all I could say
is if I could I would write
you some way out of this—
but my gift is useless.

And you said
no.

Write me a poem to
make me happy.

So I wrote.

Move pen move—
Write me a bedroom
where cures make love
to our cancers.

But my mother just motions
to a bottle full of answers and says
help me go.

And now I know something of how
a piano must feel when it looks at the fireplace
to see sheet music being used for kindling
smoke signaling the end of some song
that I thought it would take too long
to learn.

Now I just sit here watching
you burn away all those notes
I never had a chance to play
to hear the music of what
you had to say.

I count out the pills
just to see if I can do it.
I can't even get halfway
through it before I turn back
into your son and say
stay.

I could hook up my heart to your ears
and let my tears be your morphine drip
because maybe it's easier to let you slip
away than it is to say
goodbye.

So I hold
my breath.

Because in the count down to death
the question of why
melts into when.

How much time do we have left?
because if I knew what I
know now then...

Move pen move—
write me a mountain.

Because headstones are not big enough.

my mother says
stop it.
Write me a poem
to make me happy.

So I write
stay.

she smiles and says
gotta go.

I know.

Goodbye.

Whatever Mountain

If you think it will be easy...

If you think the path will be
laid out before you or that the
trail will have previously been
blazed, all obstacles cleared, every
footstep already pioneered by those
who have gone before you...

If you think that every barricade
will have been dismantled
or that every wall will
have been removed...

If you think pressing your hands
into the wet cement of a foundation
will have proved to the world
you have left your mark upon it...

If you think the grit under your fingernails
is evidence that you have done enough,
or that your rough and callused hands
offer sufficient testimony that
you have earned rest...

If you think the test will be anything less
than an essay question aimed at
unearthing the answer of how
much your heart can bear...

you will be disappointed.

It will require more than that.

There will be no welcome mat waiting
to greet you at the foot of this
mountain, no medal to pin upon
your chest when this is done.

You will have won nothing
by crossing this finish line.

It exists only to task you with
discovering how much
deeper you can go.

It will insist that you drill past
the *I don't know* that has stood
stubbornly in your way since the
instant you first wondered if you could.

It will burden you with the charge
of bringing to the surface an understanding
of the misunderstood, the excavation
of an answer to the question—

What now?

How do you keep going
in a world where the hellos
are outweighed by the goodbyes?

How do you train yourself to know
that you have to battle through the fall
if you ever expect to rise?

You have to accept the fact that the size of
the mountain in front of you is secondary
to the fact that there is a mountain
in your way.

Now, what are you going to do?

You don't need a finish line
to remind you that the way forward
exists because of the work you put in
forging the path behind you.

Effort isn't weighed on scales.

There will be times when the last
breath in your lungs must volunteer
to become the wind in your sails.

Because who else is going to do it?

Forward
            forward
                        forward
faster than full speed toward the
colossus of uncertainty that's been laying
bricks in your throat to make room
for the quiet impostor sent
to replace your roar.

Your strength is not diminished
because others think your struggle is futile.

Every time you broke
you learned to reconcile the pieces
and build a better self, using what you
could salvage from the ruins of your slaughter.

Your alma mater was a school of thought
where the lessons were taught in reverse—

test first
            instruction later.

It was a classroom
dedicated to the teaching
of what can be learned from your failure.

The answers were never
meant to be easy.

You've always known it.

You don't borrow the conviction it takes
to make yourself practice the impossible—

      you own it.

The heaviest things we will ever
have to lift are our own spirits.

They will at times
be weighed down with
the terrible gravity that is doubt

They will at times refuse to man
the lighthouse meant to steer
you clear from disaster.

You will never master being whole
without first knowing that some of the pieces
we lose stay lost, and that sometimes
the cost of moving forward is having
to leave behind that part of yourself
and learn to exist without it.

To face down whatever mountain
is in your way and then

do what you're going to
do about it.

ACKNOWLEDGEMENTS

About the Author

Canadian poet and spoken-word artist Shane Koyczan was born in Yellowknife, Northwest Territories, to a French mother and a father of First Nations heritage. He grew up in Penticton, British Columbia, and was educated at Okanagan College.

In his poems, Koyczan uses personal narrative to engage themes of social justice, mental health, and love. He is a member of the "talk rock" band Short Story Long and the spoken-word group Tons of Fun University (TOFU).

Winner of both the individual champion title at the National Poetry Slam and the Canadian Spoken Word Olympics, Koyczan performed his poem "We Are More" at the opening ceremonies for the 2010 Vancouver Olympics. For his social justice work, Koyczan received a BC Civil Liberties Award for the Arts. ShaneKoyczan.com

If You Like Shane Koyczan Shane Likes...

My Soft Response To The Wars
RC Weslowski

Undisputed Greatest Writer Of All Time
Beau Sia

Bring Down The Chandeliers
Tara Hardy

Other Books by Shane:

Visiting Hours

Stickboy

Our Deathbeds Will Be Thirsty

A Bruise On Light

Silence Is A Song I Know All The Words To

Turn On A Light

To This Day

Inconvenient Skin

The Basement In My Attic

Upcoming releases:

Touch Is A Vitamin

First Time Again

Write Bloody Books

After the Witch Hunt — Megan Falley
Aim for the Head: An Anthology of Zombie Poetry — Rob Sturma, Editor
Allow The Light: The Lost Poems of Jack McCarthy — Jessica Lohafer, Editor
Amulet — Jason Bayani
Any Psalm You Want — Khary Jackson
Atrophy — Jackson Burgess
Birthday Girl with Possum — Brendan Constantine
The Bones Below — Sierra DeMulder
Born in the Year of the Butterfly Knife — Derrick C. Brown
Bouquet of Red Flags — Taylor Mali
Bring Down the Chandeliers — Tara Hardy
Ceremony for the Choking Ghost — Karen Finneyfrock
A Constellation of Half-Lives — Seema Reza
Counting Descent — Clint Smith
Courage: Daring Poems for Gutsy Girls — Karen Finneyfrock, Mindy Nettifee, & Rachel McKibbens, Editors
Cut to Bloom — Arhm Choi Wild
Dear Future Boyfriend — Cristin O'Keefe Aptowicz
Do Not Bring Him Water — Caitlin Scarano
Don't Smell the Floss — Matty Byloos
Drive Here and Devastate Me — Megan Falley
Drunks and Other Poems of Recovery — Jack McCarthy
The Elephant Engine High Dive Revival — Derrick C. Brown, Editor
Every Little Vanishing — Sheleen McElhinney
Everyone I Love Is a Stranger to Someone — Annelyse Gelman
Everything Is Everything — Cristin O'Keefe Aptowicz
Favorite Daughter — Nancy Huang
The Feather Room — Anis Mojgani
Floating, Brilliant, Gone — Franny Choi
Glitter in the Blood: A Poet's Manifesto for Better, Braver Writing — Mindy Nettifee
Gold That Frames the Mirror — Brandon Melendez

The Heart of a Comet — Pages D. Matam

Heavy Lead Birdsong — Ryler Dustin

Heirloom — Ashia Ajani

Here I Am Burn Me — Kimberly Nguyen

Her Whole Bright Life — Courtney LeBlanc

Hello. It Doesn't Matter. — Derrick C. Brown

Help in the Dark Season — Jacqueline Suskin

Hot Teen Slut — Cristin O'Keefe Aptowicz

How the Body Works the Dark — Derrick C. Brown

How to Love the Empty Air — Cristin O'Keefe Aptowicz

I Love Science! — Shanny Jean Maney

I Love You Is Back — Derrick C. Brown

The Importance of Being Ernest — Ernest Cline

The Incredible Sestina Anthology — Daniel Nester, Editor

In Search of Midnight — Mike McGee

In the Pockets of Small Gods — Anis Mojgani

Junkyard Ghost Revival — Derrick C. Brown, Editor

Keep Your Little Lights Alive —John-Francis Quiñonez

Kissing Oscar Wilde — Jade Sylvan

The Last American Valentine — Derrick C. Brown, Editor

The Last Time as We Are — Taylor Mali

Learn Then Burn — Tim Stafford & Derrick C. Brown, Editors

Learn Then Burn Teacher's Guide — Tim Stafford & Molly Meacham, Editors

Learn Then Burn 2: This Time It's Personal — Tim Stafford, Editor

Lessons on Being Tenderheaded — Janae Johnson

Love Ends In A Tandem Kayak — Derrick C. Brown

Love in a Time of Robot Apocalypse — David Perez

The Madness Vase — Andrea Gibson

Multiverse: An Anthology of Superhero Poetry of Superhuman Proportions —
Rob Sturma & Ryk McIntyre, Editors

My, My, My, My, My — Tara Hardy

The New Clean — Jon Sands

New Shoes on a Dead Horse — Sierra DeMulder

Open Your Mouth like a Bell — Mindy Nettifee
Ordinary Cruelty — Amber Flame
Our Poison Horse — Derrick C. Brown
Over the Anvil We Stretch — Anis Mojgani
Pansy — Andrea Gibson
Pecking Order — Nicole Homer
The Pocketknife Bible — Anis Mojgani
Pole Dancing to Gospel Hymns — Andrea Gibson
Racing Hummingbirds — Jeanann Verlee
Reasons to Leave the Slaughter — Ben Clark
Redhead and the Slaughter King — Megan Falley
Rise of the Trust Fall — Mindy Nettifee
Said the Manic to the Muse — Jeanann Verlee
Scandalabra — Derrick C. Brown
Slow Dance with Sasquatch — Jeremy Radin
The Smell of Good Mud — Lauren Zuniga
Some of the Children Were Listening — Lauren Sanderson
Songs from Under the River — Anis Mojgani
Strange Light — Derrick C. Brown
The Tigers, They Let Me — Anis Mojgani
Thin Ice Olympics — Jeffery McDaniel
38 Bar Blues — C.R. Avery
This Way to the Sugar — Hieu Minh Nguyen
Time Bomb Snooze Alarm — Bucky Sinister
Uh-Oh — Derrick C. Brown
Uncontrolled Experiments in Freedom — Brian S. Ellis
The Undisputed Greatest Writer of All Time — Beau Sia
The Way We Move Through Water — Lino Anunciacion
We Will Be Shelter — Andrea Gibson, Editor
What Learning Leaves — Taylor Mali
What the Night Demands — Miles Walser
Working Class Represent — Cristin O'Keefe Aptowicz
Workin' Mime to Five — Dick Richards

www.ingramcontent.com/pod-product-compliance
Ingram Content Group UK Ltd.
Pitfield, Milton Keynes, MK11 3LW, UK
UKHW041028090625
6300UKWH00038B/464

9 780984 503179